LEGO STAR WARS

IMPERIAL FORCES

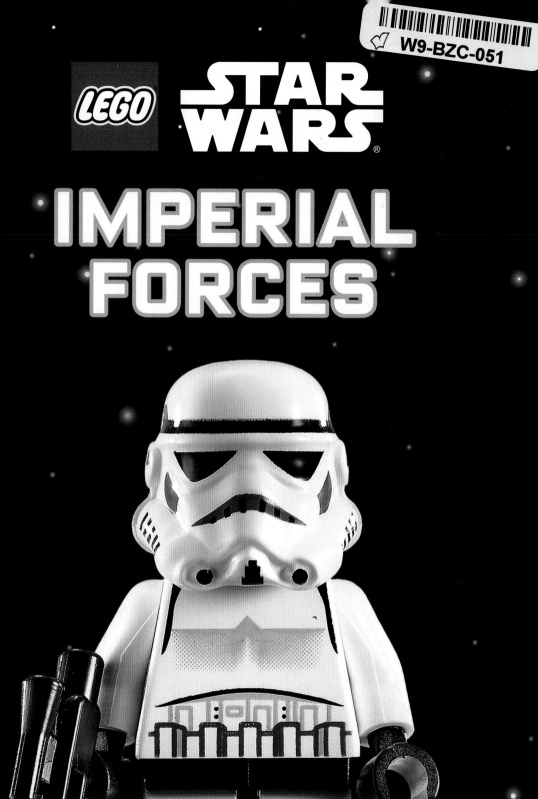

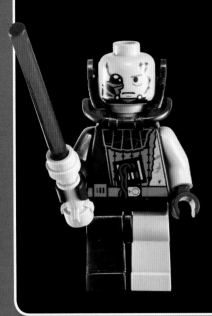

INTRODUCTION

The terrifying Empire rules the LEGO® *Star Wars* galaxy with an iron fist. Learn all about their army of minifigures—from the cunning Grand Moff Tarkin to the tiny mouse droid.

HOW TO USE THIS BOOK

These amazing minifigures are ordered according to the *Star Wars*® property in which they first appeared or mostly featured. Tabs at the top of each page indicate which properties this minifgure appears in. As most Star Wars characters appear in the Expanded Universe, that tab is highlighted only if a minifigure appears in an EU set. The Clone Wars tab has not been highlighted if the character has a separate Clone Wars minifigure.

This book also includes variants of featured minifigures, which are the same character, but have some modifications that make them different in some way.

Introduction
MEET THE MINIFIGURES

Contents

Emperor Palpatine
DARK DICTATOR

Sith Lord Emperor Palpatine is the self-appointed ruler of the LEGO *Star Wars* galaxy. His minifigure dresses in simple black robes, and three variants carry a cane to make him look weak, but don't be fooled! This is a man of terrible power who has made his presence felt in seven LEGO sets.

STAR VARIANT
The first Emperor
The original Emperor Palpatine minifigure has different printing on his torso, yellow hands, and a yellow face with smaller (but no less terrifying!) eyes. He also walks with a cane. The variant is in three 2000–2002 sets.

Black hood hides Palpatine's face, which has been distorted by dark side energies

Lightning strike
Emperor Palpatine's red-bladed lightsaber is not his only powerful weapon. The minifigure lashes out at Luke Skywalker with deadly Force lightning on the LEGO Death Star (set 10188)!

Red-bladed Sith lightsaber

Palpatine acquired this unique gray, wrinkled LEGO head with large, staring Sith eyes in the 2008 redesign

Palpatine's black robe printing was first seen on the 2008 redesign. Only this minifigure has this torso piece

Black hands—a variant in the Imperial Inspection (set 7264) has gray hands

Hologram

The Imperial Star Destroyer (set 6211) features Emperor Palpatine's minifigure as a hologram. His printed image appears on a sticker attached to a transparent-blue LEGO brick.

DATA FILE
SET: 8096 Emperor Palpatine's Shuttle
YEAR: 2010
PIECES: 5
EQUIPMENT: Cape, lightsaber
VARIANTS: 4

STAR VARIANTS

Lighting the way
2005 saw the addition of light-up lightsabers to the LEGO *Star Wars* theme. Vader's appears in TIE Fighter (set 7263) with a minifigure that uses the original Vader torso design.

Chrome Vader
Vader's black suit took on a chrome sheen for a special figure for the 10th Anniversary of LEGO *Star Wars* in 2009.

Darth Vader's iconic look is instantly recognizable in his LEGO minifigure form. There are nine variants, all made up of combinations of two torso designs, a cape, and four heads (with variations in the eyebrows, eye color, and scar patterns), but just one trademark helmet piece.

Intimidating red Sith lightsaber

Removable helmet piece is common to all Vader minifigures and was first molded in 1999

Whites of his eyes
In 2009, Vader's previously black eyes received white pupils for the first time.

The second Vader torso design, first seen in 2008, has a detailed control chestplate and a utility belt

Welcome to Toy Fair
The anniversary-edition chrome-black Darth Vader minifigure was given out to lucky guests at the 2009 Toy Fair in New York in a special LEGO Collectors Event presentation box.

Darth Vader
SITH LORD

DATA FILE
SET: 10212 Imperial Shuttle
YEAR: 2010
PIECES: 5
EQUIPMENT: Cape, lightsaber
VARIANTS: 9

Medical droids are programmed to help anyone in need, and this multi-armed medic is responsible for bringing Darth Vader back from the brink of death. FX-6 saves the Sith's damaged body and encases it in the life-support uniform for which Vader becomes famous. This minifigure is exclusive to one LEGO set and is the only minifigure to incorporate the cone piece.

Darth Vader Transformation (set 7251)
On Coruscant, FX-6 toils away in secret. On one side of the rotatable operating table is Anakin's injured minifigure. On the other is Vader, resplendent in his new shiny suit.

DATA FILE

SET: 7251 Darth Vader Transformation
YEAR: 2005
PIECES: 21
EQUIPMENT: Closed-wrench, hammer, power drill, screwdriver, wrench
VARIANTS: 1

FX-6
MEDICAL ASSISTANT DROID

Data bank provides robot with medical knowledge

Toy Fair toy
FX-6 also appears in an exclusive VIP Gala edition of Darth Vader Transformation (set 7251), which was given out to guests at the 2005 LEGO International Toy Fair in New York.

Rotatable five-armed droid is an expert at multitasking

Classic tools from various other LEGO themes are used to repair Vader's body and forge his metal suit

Broad cone base gives droid stability during delicate surgical procedures

STAR VARIANTS

Leg armor
This stormtrooper variant has an extension of his utilty belt and armor shin plates on his hips and legs. The 2005 minifigure is exclusive to Imperial Inspection (set 7264).

Silver-trooper
This shiny chrome silver stormtrooper was released in a promotional polybag in 2010. It was sold exclusively at Toys 'R' Us stores throughout March of that year.

Reinforced helmet with internal comlink

Loyal to the Empire and highly disciplined, a stormtrooper is built to succeed in combat. Shielded in white space armor, these nameless soldiers have blank heads beneath their helmets to ensure anonymity. Seven stormtrooper variants have appeared in 15 sets since 2001.

Heads up
All seven variants of the stormtrooper minifigure have blank heads but the colors vary. The two earliest variants have yellow heads, two others have light flesh heads, and the three latest variants have black heads.

Dotted mouth grilles have been seen on stormtroopers from the 2007 sets onwards

DATA FILE
SET: 10212 Imperial Shuttle
YEAR: 2010
PIECES: 4
EQUIPMENT: Blaster
VARIANTS: 7

Utility belt with blaster power cell reserves

E-11 blaster pistol with rangefinder

Back armor
A stormtrooper has emergency breathing apparatus and a thermal detonator on the back of his armor.

Stormtrooper
IMPERIAL SOLDIER

These droids are programmed to perform specific tasks in the LEGO *Star Wars* galaxy, providing the LEGO minifigures with various forms of help. Some are used for maintenance work, some provide energy, and some—like the Imperial IT-0 interrogator droid—are used for far more sinister ends!

Droids
MECHANICAL HELPERS

Probing arm is a LEGO screwdriver piece

The IT-0 records all information obtained during interrogations

DATA FILE
NAME: IT-0
ROLE: Imperial interrogator
SET: 10188 Death Star
YEAR: 2008
PIECES: 9
VARIANTS: 1

The IT-0 has a light bluish-gray LEGO stand so it appears to hover in the air

DATA FILE
NAME: Sentry droid
ROLE: Imperial surveillance
SET: 8092 Luke's Landspeeder
YEAR: 2010
PIECES: 8
VARIANTS: 1

Communications antenna

The sentry droid hovers off the ground on a translucent LEGO stand

The mouse droid is used on the Death Star (set 10188) and the Imperial Star Destroyer (set 6211)

DATA FILE
NAME: Mouse droid
ROLE: Imperial messenger
SET: 10188 Death Star
YEAR: 2008
PIECES: 9
VARIANTS: 1

Gray plate piece has a ring clip to attach the wheels

STAR VARIANT

Orange pauldron

Sandtrooper squad leaders and commanders wear orange shoulder pauldrons over their armor. This sandtrooper variant appears in Mos Eisley Cantina (set 4501).

Helmet is the same as that of a regular LEGO stormtrooper (p.9)

The sandtrooper minifigure might look a lot like a stormtrooper, but his armor has been specifically adapted to withstand extreme desert climates found on planets like Tatooine. Commander and regular officer sandtrooper minifigures have appeared in LEGO *Star Wars* sets since 2003.

DATA FILE

SET: 8092 Luke's Landspeeder
YEAR: 2010
PIECES: 11
EQUIPMENT: Blaster, pauldron
VARIANTS: 4

Helmet has inbuilt breathing filters to withstand the fierce desert sun

Pauldron cloths denote rank. Regular sandtroopers wear black pauldrons

Blaster gun. Mounted sandtroopers carry long electropikes in Mos Eisley Cantina (set 4501)

Sandtrooper armor has an inbuilt cooling system

Sandtrooper
DESERT SOLDIER

Rebreather

Sandtroopers wear rebreather packs to regulate their oxygen supply in sweltering desert climes.

Imperial Officer
THE EMPEROR'S HENCHMAN

Wearing a starched gray uniform, the Imperial officer minifigure is part of the Emperor's vast army. These high-ranking soldiers work far from the battlefield, aboard starships like the Imperial Shuttle (set 10212). First appearing in 2002 with an unusually cheery smile, the Imperial officer became more stern in 2010.

Dark bluish-gray Imperial officer kepi

STAR VARIANT

First officer
This original variant is only in the 2002 set Final Duel II (set 7201). He has a sunnier disposition than his 2010 counterpart! Before the 2010 redesign, all Imperial officer minifigures had smiling faces.

Kepi
Many members of the LEGO *Star Wars* security forces wear a flat, circular cap with a peak called a kepi. The same kepi is worn in gray by Admiral Piett (p.18), in black by the Imperial pilot (p.22) and Juno Eclipse, and in blue by the Bespin guard.

The Imperial officer has a stern expression because he takes his work for the Empire very seriously. The Hoth Rebel trooper and Hoth Imperial officer (p.19) have the same head

Imperial code cylinder—only important military officers carry these sophisticated keycards

Red and blue rank insignia plaque

Dark bluish-gray tunic. All Imperial officer variants wear this uniform print, but the original, from Final Duel II (set 7201), has it in darker gray

Imperial officer minifigures carry no weapons because they work away from the battlefield

DATA FILE
SET: 10212 Imperial Shuttle
YEAR: 2010
PIECES: 4
EQUIPMENT: None
VARIANTS: 4

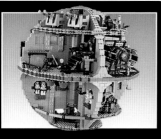

Death Star (set 10188)
The Death Star droid is exclusive to this set. If in need of repairs, the Death Star droid can take the turbolift to the Death Star's droid maintenance room (top right in picture). The facility has a work bench and tool rack.

Photoreceptors are a droid's visual organs. The RA-7 uses his to spy on officials

This RA-7 protocol droid is informally known as a Death Star droid because its kind is generally found on the Imperial battle station. The droids look like C-3PO, but they are very different: They have low intelligence and are programmed to be stern rather than helpful. The RA-7 is exclusive to the Death Star (set 10188), where its main role is to spy on officials like Grand Moff Tarkin.

Vocabulator allows the RA-7 to speak—and pass on secrets

Head start
The protocol droid head piece on the Death Star droid minifigure was first created for C-3PO in 2000. The head piece can also be found on fellow protocol droids R-3PO, and K-3PO.

Primary power outlet

Printed chest plate. The same print is used on C-3PO, R-3PO, and K-3PO and continues on the back

Death Star Droid
RA-7 PROTOCOL DROID

DATA FILE
SET: 10188 Death Star
YEAR: 2008
PIECES: 3
EQUIPMENT: None
VARIANTS: 1

These elite pilots of the Imperial Navy are referred to as "bucketheads" by Rebel pilots because of their bulky helmets. Their unique headgear and flight suits are a self-contained life-support system that helps them survive in the vacuum of space. The TIE pilot minifigure has fought in five sets since 2001.

This custom TIE helmet is first seen in 2010. It is the same mold as the white helmet worn by the AT-AT driver minifigure (p.21)

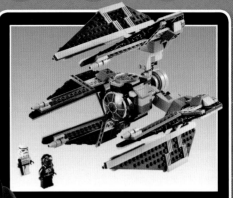

TIE Defender (set 8087)
The redesigned TIE pilot has only appeared in the 2010 set TIE Defender (set 8087). The minifigure has no seat or controls in the starfighter's cramped cockpit, but it rotates as the starfighter twists and turns in battle.

STAR VARIANT

Imperial helmet
Before 2010, the TIE pilot's helmet was the same design as the stormtrooper helmet (p.9). This original variant appears in two LEGO sets: TIE Fighter (set 7146) and TIE Bomber (set 4479).

TIE Pilot
ELITE IMPERIAL PILOT

Breather tubes transfer oxygen

The TIE pilot has worn this unique torso piece since its 2001 debut. The life-support chest piece helps the pilot adapt for changing altitudes

Hidden heads
A peek under the oversized helmet of the latest TIE pilot reveals a plain black head. A 2006 variant of the minifigure also has a black head, but the two earlier variants have brown and reddish-brown heads.

DATA FILE
SET: 8087 TIE Defender
YEAR: 2010
PIECES: 4
EQUIPMENT: None
VARIANTS: 4

Death Star (set 10188)
Grand Moff Tarkin is one of 24 minifigures included in the LEGO Death Star. Inside the superlaser control room, Tarkin just needs to say the word and the Death Star's powerful superweapon can fire a laser beam powerful enough to destroy an entire planet.

Governer of the Imperial Outland Regions, Grand Moff Tarkin has appeared in two LEGO *Star Wars* sets since 2006. Both sets—Imperial Star Destroyer (6211) and Death Star (10188)—are jewels in the Empire's fleet, while Tarkin's intimidating countenance and obvious rank make him one of the Empire's most feared men.

Standard short LEGO hair in light bluish-gray. The same piece is used on Owen Lars and old Obi Wan "Ben" Kenobi in the LEGO *Star Wars* theme

Light flesh head with drawn cheekbones and a scowl is unique to Grand Moff Tarkin

Imperial code cylinders. High-ranking Tarkin keeps one of these important security devices on each side of his tunic

Unique rank badge indicates military status. As Grand Moff, Tarkin has two rows of colored squares

Black belt with silver Imperial officer's disc

Grand Moff Tarkin
IMPERIAL GOVERNER

DATA FILE
SETS: 10188 Death Star
YEAR: 2008
PIECES: 4
EQUIPMENT: None
VARIANTS: 1

With a stern countenance and full black attire, the Death Star guard is a deliberately intimidating minifigure. He is part of a handpicked, elite fighting force that can handle any number of combat and non-combat roles for the Imperial Navy, appearing aboard the LEGO Death Star (set 10188) and at The Battle of Endor (set 8038).

Death Star (set 10188)

Aboard the LEGO Death Star, two elite Death Star guard minifigures control the mechanism for the superlaser firing dish. The huge laser is ready to destroy anything in its path at Darth Vader's command.

Death Star Guard

FEARSOME FIGHTER

With its extended neck guard, the Death Star guard's helmet bears a resemblance to that worn by Darth Vader (p.7)

Black attack
The Death Star guard is the only LEGO minifigure to wear his helmet in black. However this style is popular with other Imperial minifigures: General Veers (p.19) and the Imperial AT-ST driver (p.20) wear it in gray tones.

The Rebel trooper also has this LEGO head with printed black chin guard

The Death Star guard wears the same torso as the Imperial pilot (p.22). It features a black imperial tunic and utility belt

Black gloves complete the all-black look

The minifigure has a LEGO blaster to use when he requires it, but for many of his duties he remains unarmed

DATA FILE
SET: 8038 The Battle of Endor
YEAR: 2009
PIECES: 4
EQUIPMENT: Blaster
VARIANTS: 1

DATA FILE

SET: 7666 Hoth Rebel Base
YEAR: 2007
PIECES: 21
EQUIPMENT: None
VARIANTS: 1

High-frequency transmission antenna is a small LEGO lever piece also seen on the destroyer droid, and the sentry droid, R1-G4

This mysterious minifigure is an Imperial probe droid. If you have spotted it, it has probably already spotted you, so watch out for its blaster fire! The LEGO Imperial probe droid carries out reconnaisance missions for the Empire, seeking out its target's secrets. The minifigure has only ever been seen in one LEGO set.

Black armored head is equipped with photoreceptors and transmitters around its circumference

The probe droid's sensor eyes survey large areas. This one has lit up—perhaps it has detected something!

These black mechanical arms are also seen on the elite assassin droid

Floating foe
The Imperial probe droid floats above the ground on repulsorlift engines in the *Star Wars* movies. Its LEGO counterpart is raised on a translucent-and-white stand so it looks to be hovering off the snowy ground of Hoth.

An inverted white dish piece makes a stable base for the Imperial probe droid

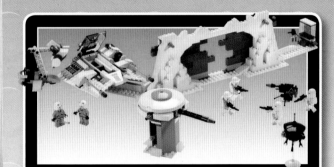

Hoth Rebel Base (set 7666)
The Imperial probe droid has discovered the secret Rebel base on Hoth! It communicates its findings to Imperial forces and the Battle of Hoth begins. The Imperial probe droid is exclusive to this limited-edition set, released in 2007.

Imperial Probe Droid
ROVING RECONNAISSANCE

Admiral Firmus Piett is the intelligent, but secretly incompetent, admiral of the Ultimate Super Star Destroyer (set 10221). He is skilled at avoiding conflict with Darth Vader by staying under the radar—much like his LEGO minifigure, which has long been absent from the LEGO *Star Wars* galaxy.

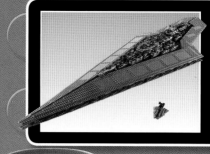

Ultimate Super Star Destroyer (set 10221)

Admiral Piett's first and only LEGO appearance is in this set from 2011. In it, he commands the imposing Star Dreadnought *Executor* warship.

Admiral Firmus Piett
IMPERIAL ADMIRAL

Unwanted guests

Piett must sit with three bounty hunters on board the *Executor*, even though he considers them to be "scum."

Piett wears a dark gray cap called a kepi atop his stern, humorless face

Admiral Piett's insignia displays his high rank on the front of his unique torso

Piett's minimal gray tunic enhances his austere image

Piett's belt buckle has an Imperial silver officer's disk that can store top secret data

DATA FILE

SET: 10221 Ultimate Super Star Destroyer
YEAR: 2011
PIECES: 4
EQUIPMENT: None
VARIANTS: 1

Back to back

Admiral Piett is the first Imperial officer to feature printed details on the back of his torso. The Imperial officer minifigure (p.12) and even powerful Grand Moff Tarkin (p.15) do not have printing depicting the backs of their gray uniforms.

STAR VARIANT

In an AT-AT
The Motorized Walking AT-AT (set 10178) from 2007 includes this variant of General Veers. He wears darker gray headgear plus goggles and a chin-strap. He does not wear black gloves in this LEGO set.

Ruthless and aggressive, Veers is the Major General of the Empire's Imperial Army. He leads the assault on Hoth and helps Darth Vader to capture Echo Base with his AT-AT Walker (set 8129). Parts of his minifigure are seen on other Imperial LEGO minifigures, but his disdainful facial expression remains unique to General Veers.

The 2010 variant has no chin-strap or goggles, so you can see his chin dimple

Light gray, cowl-like helmet piece also appears on the Hoth Imperial officer from the Snowtrooper Battle Pack (set 8084).

Smiles Ahead
The Hoth Imperial officer is exactly the same minifigure, except for his more smiley face.

This variant of General Veers wears a detailed armor pack. The 2007 variant wears a plain officer tunic

Veers's torso pack can also be seen on the Hoth Imperial officer. The red and blue stripes near his left shoulder denote military rank

General Veers wears black flight gloves for piloting the AT-AT walker

Backplate
Veers's LEGO torso piece shows straps connecting the front and back armor plates.

DATA FILE
SET: 8129 AT-AT Walker
YEAR: 2010
PIECES: 4
EQUIPMENT: None
VARIANTS: 2

General Veers
IMPERIAL GENERAL

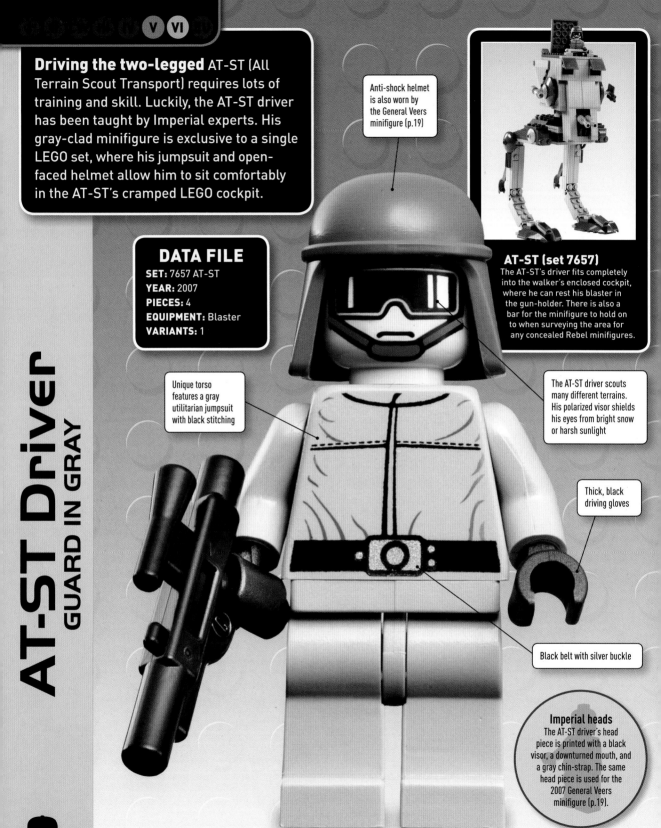

Driving the two-legged AT-ST (All Terrain Scout Transport) requires lots of training and skill. Luckily, the AT-ST driver has been taught by Imperial experts. His gray-clad minifigure is exclusive to a single LEGO set, where his jumpsuit and open-faced helmet allow him to sit comfortably in the AT-ST's cramped LEGO cockpit.

Anti-shock helmet is also worn by the General Veers minifigure (p.19)

AT-ST (set 7657)
The AT-ST's driver fits completely into the walker's enclosed cockpit, where he can rest his blaster in the gun-holder. There is also a bar for the minifigure to hold on to when surveying the area for any concealed Rebel minifigures.

DATA FILE
SET: 7657 AT-ST
YEAR: 2007
PIECES: 4
EQUIPMENT: Blaster
VARIANTS: 1

AT-ST Driver
GUARD IN GRAY

Unique torso features a gray utilitarian jumpsuit with black stitching

The AT-ST driver scouts many different terrains. His polarized visor shields his eyes from bright snow or harsh sunlight

Thick, black driving gloves

Black belt with silver buckle

Imperial heads
The AT-ST driver's head piece is printed with a black visor, a downturned mouth, and a gray chin-strap. The same head piece is used for the 2007 General Veers minifigure (p.19).

STAR VARIANT

Helmet

The AT-AT driver minifigure from Motorized Walking AT-AT (set 10178) has a smaller helmet. It is the same LEGO piece used for stormtrooper helmets, but with specially designed AT-AT markings (p.9).

Life-support back

The printed back of the AT-AT driver's torso reveals the life-support's oxygen pack, which contains emergency supplies.

Helmet is marked with Imperial symbols

The AT-AT driver is a top Imperial soldier. His minifigure commands a deadly AT-AT (All Terrain Armored Transport) walker. Three variations of the AT-AT driver have appeared in four LEGO sets since 2003. His minifigure wears a gray jumpsuit under blaster-proof armor. He also has a unique, specialized helmet.

Specialized AT-AT helmet has a breathing apparatus that enables the driver to breathe on any land-based terrain he explores

The unique torso's life-support system connects the air supply to the helmet through two tubes

Energy monitor

Identity chip

The AT-AT driver wears a light-gray harness

AT-AT Driver
ALL TERRAIN TERROR

DATA FILE

SET: 8129 AT-AT Walker
YEAR: 2010
PIECES: 4
EQUIPMENT: Blaster
VARIANTS: 3

Imperial pilots
The AT-AT driver is sometimes considered to be a pilot, even though AT-ATs are not flying machines. He shares his helmet piece with another Imperial pilot: the TIE pilot (p.14), who has a black version of the helmet and a similar torso.

The **Imperial pilot** transports many high-ranking officials aboard the Imperial shuttle. He is always dressed in his freshly pressed black uniform and cap because his next passenger might be Darth Vader—or even the Emperor himself! This minifigure has piloted the Imperial shuttle in two LEGO sets since 2001.

STAR VARIANT

Happy pilot

The original variant of this minifigure has a yellow head with the basic LEGO smiling face. He also wears an all-black uniform, but with much less detail. This rare, cheerful pilot only appears in the 2001 set Imperial Shuttle (set 7166).

Black cap is also worn by another Imperial pilot, Juno Eclipse

This pilot takes his job very seriously

On both sides

The Imperial pilot's fierce, flesh-colored head appears on both sides of the Empire/Rebel conflict. It is used for the Hoth Imperial officer (p.19), as well as for the Hoth Rebel trooper minifigure.

Torso is also used for the Death Star guard minifigure (p.16)

Imperial Shuttle (set 10212)

The Imperial pilot and three other minifigures can all fit into the spacious cockpit of the 2010 Imperial shuttle. Now the pilot can transport his Sith Masters in style!

The Imperial pilot does not fly battle craft, so he does not require the life-support equipment that LEGO TIE pilots wear (p.14). His uniform is a plain black suit with a black, blaster-proof vest

Belt holds several small storage pouches

Imperial Pilot
MAN IN BLACK

DATA FILE

SET: 10212 Imperial Shuttle
YEAR: 2010
PIECES: 4
EQUIPMENT: None
VARIANTS: 2

The mysterious Royal Guard is the Emperor's deadly personal bodyguard. The minifigure is dressed in a full crimson uniform and cape. Even his hands and eyes are concealed. In his bright and otherworldly uniform, the Royal Guard stands out among other minifigures. His presence will make any minifigure think twice about attacking the Emperor!

Imperial Inspection (set 7264)

In their crimson uniforms, the Royal Guards stand out from other Imperial soldiers in Imperial Inspection. The Royal Guard minifigures in this 2005 set are identical to the 2008 variant, except that they have red hands.

Unique hood mold was designed especially for the Royal Guard

Standard black LEGO head piece makes it look like the Royal Guard minifigure is wearing a black visor

Standard LEGO spear is used as a force pike, which employs vibrating energy to stun opponents

Black combat gloves

The Royal Guard is the only LEGO *Star Wars* minifigure to wear a red LEGO cloth cape

Royal Guard
CRIMSON PROTECTOR

DATA FILE

SET: 10188 Death Star
YEAR: 2008
PIECES: 5
EQUIPMENT: Force pike, cape
VARIANTS: 2

R2-Q5 is an astromech droid with a secret. His black and bronze minifigure has been fitted with Imperial spying technology, so he is not to be trusted! Two variants of R2-Q5's astromech minifigure have appeared in two sets since 2006: He works aboard the Death Star (set 10188) and the Imperial Star Destroyer (set 6211).

STAR VARIANT

Original R2-Q5

The original variant of R2-Q5 comes with Imperial Star Destroyer (set 6211). This 2006 R2-Q5 has an identical body piece to the 2008 minifigure, but features less printing on the domed head piece.

R2-Q5
DEVIOUS DROID

DATA FILE
SET: 10188 Death Star
YEAR: 2008
PIECES: 4
EQUIPMENT: None
VARIANTS: 2

Identity crisis
When R2-Q5 was first released as a LEGO minifigure in Imperial Star Destroyer (set 6211) in 2006, the astromech droid was incorrectly labeled as "R2-D5" on the box.

Radar eye can record surroundings

Head piece is unique to the 2008 variant

R2-Q5 is printed with all the familiar tools and access panels of a typical astromech droid, but he also contains hidden spy devices

Holographic projector reveals his secret findings

R2-Q5 is the only minifigure to have black LEGO Technic leg pins

Inference pulse stabilizers

The Battle of Endor (set 8038)
The scout trooper chases Ewok and Rebel minifigures through the forest of Endor in this LEGO set. He flies a repulsorlift speeder bike, which has a lightweight blaster cannon and is easy to maneuver through thick trees.

The Imperial scout trooper is often sent on dangerous missions on his own. His minifigure wears a specialized scout helmet and white armor that is more lightweight than regular stormtrooper armor. He also carries a powerful blaster. Two variants of the scout trooper minifigure have appeared in five LEGO sets since 1999.

Black LEGO head piece is visible beneath the helmet, creating a visor effect

Electronic visor enhances the minifigure's vision

Built-in comlink system can support long-distance communication

Kashyyyk trooper
This helmet piece is used in sand-green for the Kashyyyk trooper minifigure. Kashyyyk troopers are a scouting unit based in the jungles of Kashyyyk, where they require camouflaged armor.

The scout trooper often undertakes long, solo missions. He carries survival rations with him at all times

Unique torso has dark bluish-gray printing

Scout Trooper
SOLO SENTRY

DATA FILE
SET: 7956 Endor Battle Set
YEAR: 2011
PIECES: 4
EQUIPMENT: Blaster
VARIANTS: 2

Visor head
The original scout trooper variant has a yellow head printed with a black visor. The minifigure has appeared in three sets from 1999 to 2002.

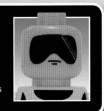

The **Imperial V-wing** pilot flies the high-speed starship during the Clone Wars, and his minifigure features elements from clone and Imperial trooper armor. He is built from the exact same pieces as the clone pilot, but with black Imperial coloring. His V-wing uniform is very similar to the TIE pilot's (p.14).

V-Wing Pilot
IMPERIAL ACE

Imperial V-Wing Starfighter (set 7915)
The V-wing pilot takes control of this starfighter and begins to fight for the growing Empire. His minifigure is exclusive to this set. The vertical-opening cockpit has no controls, but that won't stop him!

Imperial symbols

Breathing apparatus in helmet is connected to the air supply by two tubes

Self-contained armor has a life support pack that enables breathing in space

Flight mask
The V-wing pilot wears the same flight mask head piece as the clone pilot—but in black. Printed silver goggles cover his eyes.

Emergency!
A parachute and oxygen tank are printed on the back of the V-wing pilot's torso, so he is prepared for any emergency.

Utility belt is attached to the parachute on the pilot's back

DATA FILE
SET: 7915 Imperial V-Wing Starfighter
YEAR: 2011
PIECES: 4
EQUIPMENT: Blaster
VARIANTS: 1

Imperial V-Wing Starfighter (set 7915)

R2-Q5 plugs into a socket on the V-wing starfighter. The starfighter has rotating wings and an opening cockpit with controls for the pilot.

Perfect fit
In the *Star Wars* galaxy, V-wing fighters are designed to carry Q7-series droids, but in the LEGO *Star Wars* galaxy, R2-Q2 fits perfectly into the V-wing model, which he helps to navigate and repair.

Imperial droid R2-Q2 helps the V-wing pilot navigate his starship. His minifigure is built from standard LEGO astromech droid pieces but they are a unique pearlescent gray color. R2-Q2 contains the data for one the most comprehensive maps of the LEGO *Star Wars* galaxy. The Imperial army wants to keep this valuable droid safe, so he only appears in one set.

Compartment houses a periscope

R2-Q2 acquires all his data through his photoreceptor

DATA FILE
SET: 7915 Imperial V-Wing Starfighter
YEAR: 2011
PIECES: 4
EQUIPMENT: None
VARIANTS: 1

R2-Q2 uses his computer interface arm to search the *Tantive IV* for Princess Leia's hidden Death Star plans

R2-Q2 can project a hologram of his galactic map from his holoprojector

Astromech body piece is printed with the same pattern as most LEGO *Star Wars* astromech droids

Pearl light-gray leg pieces are not found in any other LEGO sets

R2-Q2
IMPERIAL ASTROMECH

Battle-damaged Darth Vader appears in one LEGO set from 2008. Other than his damaged and normal helmets, every part of his minifigure is unique to this version. His torso and face have extensive battle damage printed on them.

Repurposed
Battle-damaged Darth Vader's helmet piece is also used as a scuba diving mask or underwater visor in other LEGO themes, including Aquasharks and Hydronauts.

Normal helmet
The *Rogue Shadow* set includes Darth Vader's normal helmet as well as the battle-damaged version.

Head piece shows Vader's badly damaged face

Helmet was damaged during a fight with Galen Marek and Juno Eclipse

Darth Vader's metal suit has been ripped and broken in battle

Following a difficult battle, wires hang out of Darth Vader's torso

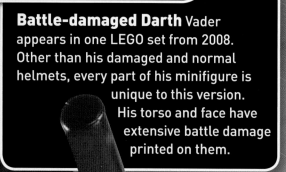

Red lightsaber with light bluish-gray hilt

This is the only *Star Wars* minifigure with one black leg and one white leg

DATA FILE

SET: 7672 *Rogue Shadow*
YEAR: 2008
PIECES: 4
EQUIPMENT: Lightsaber
VARIANTS: 1

Darth Vader SITH LORD

TIE Crawler (set 7664)
This is the first LEGO set to feature the shadow trooper. The 2007 set includes two shadow troopers, but only one can fit in the crawler's cockpit at any time. It is used for ground combat, so the other trooper can use his blaster to supplement the crawler's missiles.

The shadow trooper, also known as a Black Hole trooper, menaces in two LEGO sets. He made his debut in 2007 in the TIE Crawler (set 7664). Never before seen in the *Star Wars* movies, this shady minifigure's black head and torso pieces are not found on any other minifigure, and his mysterious name adds to his dark reputation.

Name game
In Imperial Dropship (set 7667), the shadow trooper is mistakenly named "Imperial Pilot" on the set box. In the *Star Wars* galaxy, shadow troopers have sophisticated stealth armor.

The shadow trooper has a plain black head underneath his black and blue helmet

Breathing apparatus adapts to different atmospheres

Shadow trooper armor is similar to the stormtrooper minifigure's (p.9), except it is black instead of white

Blaster gun for ground combat

Shadow Trooper
DARK STORMTROOPER

DATA FILE
SET: 7667 Imperial Dropship
YEAR: 2008
PIECES: 4
EQUIPMENT: Blaster
VARIANTS: 1

DK | Penguin Random House

Editors Hannah Dolan, Shari Last,
Victoria Taylor, and Matt Jones
Designers Anne Sharples and Jon Hall
Senior Producer Lloyd Robertson
Senior DTP Designer David McDonald
Managing Editor Simon Hugo
Design Manager Guy Harvey
Creative Manager Sarah Harland
Art Director Lisa Lanzarini
Publisher Julie Ferris
Publishing Director Simon Beecroft

Additional minifigures photographed by Huw Millington,
Ace Kim, Jeremy Beckett, and Tony Wood

First published in the United States in 2015
by DK Publishing
345 Hudson Street, New York, New York 10014

Contains material previously published in
LEGO® Star Wars® Character Encyclopedia (2011)

004-284485-Feb/15

Page design copyright ©2015 Dorling Kindersley Limited
A Penguin Random House Company

LEGO, the LEGO logo, the Brick and Knob configurations,
and the Minifigure are trademarks of the LEGO Group.
© 2015 The LEGO Group.
Produced by Dorling Kindersley Limited
under license from the LEGO Group.

© & TM 2015 LUCASFILM LTD.

A catalog record for this book is available from
the Library of Congress.

ISBN: 978-5-0010-1294-8

Color reproduction by Media Development Printing Ltd, UK
Printed and bound in China

Dorling Kindersley would like to thank:
Jonathan W. Rinzler, Troy Alders, Rayne Roberts, Pablo
Hidalgo, and Leland Chee at Lucasfilm; Stephanie
Lawrence, Randi Sørensen, Lisbeth Langjkær, Jens
Kronvold Frederiksen, Chris Bonven Johansen, and John
McCormack at the LEGO Group; LEGO Star Wars
collectors Ace Kim and Huw Millington; Emma Grange,
Lisa Stock, Sarah Harland, Ellie Hallsworth, and Nicola
Brown for editorial support; and Owen Bennett for
design support on the cover.

www.dk.com
www.LEGO.com
www.starwars.com

A WORLD OF IDEAS:
SEE ALL THERE IS TO KNOW